PTSD

Overcome The Pain,
Start Living Again

JOHN MACKEY

PTSD: Overcome the Pain, Start Living Again

2nd Edition, Copyright © 2016 by John Mackey.

Medical Disclaimer

All information provided in this book, any information relating to a particular medical condition or conditions, health care, preventive care, and/or healthy lifestyles, and is presented for general informational purposes only. This book should not be considered as a complete or exhaustive guide and does not cover all disorders or conditions or their treatment.

The information provided in this book should not be considered as a substitute for advice or recommendations provided by your own physician or health care provider. You should not use the information in this book to diagnose any health problem, disease, or to determine treatments for such conditions. You should also not use the information in this book as a substitute for professional medical advice for any health-related regimen, including diet or exercise. Always consult your own licensed health care provider for these purposes.

By downloading and/or reading this book you are declaring that you have read this statement and agree to everything it contains.

Second Edition: August 2016

ISBN: 9781520114361
Imprint: Independently published

CONTENTS

INTRODUCTION

Hello there. Thank you for purchasing this book. PTSD, also known Post-Traumatic Stress Disorder, is a serious condition. PTSD is not only limited to soldiers. Victims of child abuse, spousal abuse, and witnesses to tragic events, such as first responders, can also experience PTSD. More people with PTSD are committing suicide than ever before.

Together, we can stop this alarming trend by listening and helping those in need. Don't wait for someone else to come along; it may be too late. I hope this book helps you or a loved one.

As I write this book, I feel it is important to let you the reader know that I too suffer from PTSD. Just like you or your loved one, I can relate to the feelings, anxieties, phobias and fears that come with having to deal with these experiences.

My childhood had its challenges, resulting in me becoming a runaway teen. At such an early age, I was not yet mature enough to understand what a traumatic event was or how to seek help when one occurs. As I got out into the real world, I experienced events and situations that even to this day, are still vivid in my mind.

Experiencing traumatic events, and more importantly, the effect of these events over the long term, are handled differently by each person.

For some persons, the memories of the events can haunt their every waking moment, for their life while others can compartmentalize it away and live their everyday lives as nothing is going on.

There is no one solution for everyone. I gain therapy by sharing not only my experiences with others but also the methods and strategies I use to deal with my symptoms. I developed and wrote this book as one avenue that anyone can use to begin to learn about PTSD and where to get help.

This book is not meant to be a complete guide on PTSD, but merely a starting point for helping you, or a loved one cope with the challenges that accompany the condition.

A lot of PTSD suffers out there do not like the term Post Traumatic Stress Disorder. They would prefer it be called PTS, Post Traumatic Stress. They want to drop the Disorder part. They feel that the word Disorder degrades the condition. I would agree. What we suffer from is not a disorder, yet an actual illness. At the writing of this book, I will still refer to the condition as PTSD or Post Traumatic Stress Disorder, mainly because it is the term that most people are familiar with, however, on all future books and articles I write will have the Disorder reference dropped.

I would like to begin this book by sharing two my stories so you can understand some events that I experienced so you may have a better understanding of what can trigger PTSD. Again, not everyone will be affected the same. If reading about tragedies is too difficult for you, you may proceed directly to Chapter 1.

THE RUNAWAY AND SOLDIER

THE CARNIVAL TRAGEDY

As a sixteen-year-old runaway, I was forced to live on the streets and find work wherever I could. One of the easiest jobs to get was working for a carnival. You might think a carnival is not a place that one would experience tragedy, and I generally would agree. A carnival is usually associated with happiness and joy. However, I was not so fortunate. This a brief story that details my first major traumatic event, of many, that I would experience in my life. It haunts me even to this day, over 30 years later.

It was a Saturday. It was a hot and sunny day. I was sitting on a park bench, feeling depressed, hungry, and alone. I had just spent the last few weeks traveling on foot. I arrived in a small town in East Texas. Just inside of town, across the street from the bench where I was sitting, there was a carnival setting up. As I sat looking around, I realized that I needed to find some work soon. I went over to the carnival and found the supervisor, who was barking orders to the workers while they were setting up the rides. I asked if they had any jobs. He looked at me up and down and then stated that he needed someone to operate a game on the midway. He asked if I had any experience. I informed him I had none. He then asked my age. Even though I was only sixteen, I answered I was seventeen. He said he doubted that.

He asked if I was a runaway. I said yes, I was. He stated that he is not supposed to hire runaways, and sometimes the police would check carnivals, as they were common places to find them. I told him I had no place to go, no money for food and that I was desperate. He looked at me again, then agreed to give me a job, on the condition if the police show up looking, I must leave immediately. He offered to pay me $20 a day, plus boarding. He stated that they will be touring southern Louisiana for the next couple of months so we would not be back in Texas until after that. I told him I wanted to leave Texas anyway, so that would not be a problem. He then said that once we get to New Orleans, he knew of another carnival I could connect with, as they will tour on to Mississippi if I was looking to travel further away from Texas.

I thanked him for the job. He called over a man designated as his manager of the show. After a brief meeting, I was shown to my bunk in the "bunkhouse." The bunkhouse was an 18 wheeler trailer, with wooden beds lining each side of the trailer. They were set up 3 high. I was given a bed on the very top, in the rear of the trailer, near the door. It smelled of dirty feet. I located my bunk. It was filthy. There was just a mattress, no blankets. I had a green wool blanket with me so at least I could stay warm. I put my bag on the bunk. I went outside.

There were people all over the place, setting up rides and midway games. The carnival manager told me I would be running the ride called the Scrambler. I was surprised, I thought I would operate one of the midway games. He said that the "boss" had changed his mind. The Scrambler was a ground-based ride with four arms that formed a cross. On the end of each arm, four buckets that also formed a cross. As the ride spins, the bucket crosses turn in the opposite direction. Due to a recent arrest of the operator for outstanding warrants, there was no person to run the ride.

The manager informed me I would need to learn how to assemble and disassemble the ride before I could do anything else. He summoned a few of the other ride operators to come over and instruct me on the proper procedures. I learned that everyone that worked with the carnival needed to know how every ride and game is assembled so everyone can help each other when needed. It was surprisingly simple to assemble and operate. I checked the pins that secure the ride together. To run the ride, it merely comprised of a START and STOP button and an emergency brake. I was shown how to operate and stop the ride and emergency procedures. I performed a few test runs, and everything checked out.

At about 6 o'clock, the gates opened. I was nervous. I had never operated a carnival ride before. My first night was easy. We were to stay at this location for 2 nights. After which, we were to pack up and move to the next location. At the end of the first night, it was about 1 am when we were done cleaning up. I went to the bunk house, and as soon as I walked in, I was ambushed. I was beaten up by what seemed like everyone in the bunkhouse. I found out later that getting beaten up by the crew was a regular thing for newbies. I had a black eye, and I think I had a broken rib. Once they finished pounding on me, everything I owned was stolen. I left the bunkhouse and slept under my ride. I refused to ever sleep in the bunkhouse again.

The following morning, I went to the carnival manager and reported what happened. He told me he could do nothing with without proof of who did it. Looks like I was on my own. I prepared the ride for that night's opening. Again the night was somewhat uneventful, ordinary families coming out for a good time. We were told that after we close for the evening, we were to begin disassembling the rides and pack them up for the next town. We were going to Lake Charles, Louisiana.

The carnival gates closed at 11 o'clock. Once the patrons left, I proceeded to disassemble and pack up the Scrambler. It was quite simple. Remove 12 pins, and push the arms together. The ride folded neatly up onto the back of a tractor trailer. As I finished folding up the ride, I heard a loud commotion near the ride behind mine. The ride comprised a long slide that once disassembled, it would be mounted on two trailers. As the commotion got louder, I went over to look at what was happening. I was horrified. Once the slide was placed on the trailers, one truck would back its trailer against the other to push the second trailer onto its truck. As the first trailer was backed up to the other trailer, the ride's operator, who was guiding them was crushed between them. The carnival boss immediately knew what to do and instructed that the two trailers were not to be separated. There was a large pool of blood beneath him. An ambulance was called. He was not screaming or anything. He was conscious and talking. Once the ambulance arrived, the paramedics assessed the scene and shortly called for his wife. She worked at the carnival as well. She came within a couple of minutes and went to him.

The paramedics informed us there would be no way he would survive once they separated the trailers. The trailers acted as a tourniquet at his waist. Once separated, he would bleed out, quickly, of what blood he had left in him. After a few solemn minutes, his wife gave him a kiss and then told him she loved him. This was a difficult thing to witness. Crying and screaming, the paramedics escorted her away from the scene. As the trailers were separated, he became free, and the paramedics immediately began to feverishly work on him. He never made a sound. Amazingly, he lived for another ten minutes. I will never forget the memory of him or his grieving wife.

I had just seen a person die, right in front of me. Unfortunately, this would not be the last time I would see death. As I sat alone and sobbed quietly, I looked up and noticed that the local Sheriff had arrived. He asked to speak to everyone who saw anything. The carnival boss came over and told me I had better leave. I wanted to tell my story, but in doing so, I would expose my secret of being a runaway. He shook my hand and gave me $40 for my two days of work. I went back to my ride and gathered the few possessions I had left. I had a change of clothes and a blanket. I then went to the back of the carnival and slipped into the woods. I walked about a mile away and set up a camp for the rest of the night. I was cold, horrified and hungry. What an experience. I pondered whether I should go back home.

THE FORT SILL EXPERIENCE

The year was 1989. I enlisted in the U.S. Army. This story involves an experience I had in Basic Training that further exacerbated my PTSD.

Our bus approached the main gate of Ft. Sill, Oklahoma. It was early in the morning, around 2 am. The bus slowly followed a meandering road until we stopped in front of a large building. As the bus door opened, a large man, wearing a highly-pressed uniform with a very distinctive brown hat, entered the bus. Once inside, he paused for a second, just glaring at all of us. No one said a word. Then suddenly and in a real quiet voice, he said, "Get off my bus. You have 30 seconds".

Because of the quiet and calm tone of his voice, no one had any sense of urgency. As we would quickly learn, however, this was a mistake. A few seconds passed, then he yelled, "GET OFF MY BUS! YOU NOW HAVE 20 SECONDS!" What a shock to the senses! We scrambled off the bus, almost like a bunch of cockroaches do when a dark room is suddenly lit. We were lined up next to a curb, toe to heel. Your nose was in the hair of the man in front of you, and the man behind you had his nose in yours. Good thing, the man in front of me bathed recently.

Otherwise, this would have been horrible. We were then told to enter the building.

As soon as we passed through the double doors, we were told to go to our left and follow a maze. We were told this would be one and only time we would pass through this maze. It was the amnesty maze. Along the path, barrels were labeled for different items, guns, knives, cigarettes, alcohol, and drugs. The alcohol, cigarette, and gun barrels had the most items. We were told if we were caught with these items, we would be in serious trouble, and would face military justice. I would not risk anything, so I put the remaining 1.5 cartons of cigarettes in the right barrel. I had nothing else.

Once done with the amnesty maze, we were then seated in a large room with school desks. Once everyone was seated, we were then ordered to get up. We now took our third oath of enlistment. After our oath, we were then seated and filled out the paperwork to begin our military records. Once completed, around 4 am, we then were taken to the barber shop. My hair was rather long. I was told I should have gotten a haircut before arriving, I didn't, and boy did I pay for it. The DS made the barber shave half my head and then forced me to get in the back of the line and wait to get the other half done. I looked goofy. Once haircuts were done, we then went to another station where they placed the fake dress uniform on us and took our first picture. The fake uniform was merely a shirt, tie, and jacket that just hung on your shoulders, no back. Then the hat. Click! And that was it.

It was now close to 5 am, we were then showed our barracks. A long bay style room, with dozens of metal bunk beds. We were told to go to sleep. No one slept. My mistake was the previous night before we left, I watched the movie, Full Metal Jacket. All I could think of while lying there was the blanket party given to Private Pyle. Not sleeping mattered little, 7 am the Drill Sergeants came in and told us to get up.

We went outside, and waiting for us were the "cattle cars." These were 18 wheeler trailers, commonly used to transport cows. We were told this would be our primary mode of transportation while in Basic Training. We packed into the trailers, and they took us back to the main building areas. We stopped at the phone room where everyone was allowed one phone call to let someone know we made it ok. The call was to only last 20 seconds. We then went to uniform issue building and received our first sets of battle dress and class-a uniforms. We were then taught how to get dressed the military way and then to chow (breakfast).

Once again we lined up heel to toe, waited to get our food, then had 10 minutes to eat and get out. As a smoker, I was Jonesing for a cigarette by now. That was quickly abated, though, as we began the first session of what would become many sessions of push-ups and sit-ups. Every command issued to us was followed by us yelling at the top of our lungs, "YES DRILL SERGEANT!"

A couple of weeks had now passed, and we were getting into the routine of being soldiers. This new day was an ordinary day, just like the previous ones so far. We wake up before dawn, perform P.T. (Physical Training), shower, eat chow and then start the training day. It is September now and is still hot in southern Oklahoma. On this training day, everyone was excited. We would begin training with actual weapons. The training plan stated that we would head out to a place called the Basic Rifleman's Marksmanship range, or BRM range, sometimes called the SPOTS range. After learning about what the range comprised of, we performed maintenance and cleaning of our rifles. Soon it was approaching lunchtime.

We packed up our gear and marched towards the chow area, located further down the range. As we marched, we were informed that the chow area was about 2KM away. We marched on for about ten minutes. At this point, we were about

1KM away from the chow area. As we proceeded down a long and winding trail through what seemed like a dense forest, we all the sudden, heard a massive boom ahead. At the time, Ft. Sill was an artillery training school besides a basic training location. Hearing booms from the artillery range was a common occurrence. However, this one seemed different. Besides the BRM range, there were also various artillery ranges, located several kilometers away, and to our right. This boom was different, as it seemed to occur just ahead of us, in the direction we were marching. Rounds from the artillery range should be landing further down range from where they were fired, not in our direction.

Our Drill Sergeant barked at us to get in a what is known as a staggered formation. Each of us was to be at least five meters apart, in a zig-zag line, and double time march to the chow area. Within just a couple of minutes, we arrived at the scene of the explosion, where a 105mm artillery shell had landed right in the middle of the chow area.

Waiting for their chow, another unit had arrived, as scheduled, ahead of us. As the soldiers waited in line for their chow, the round landed, right on top of them. The scene was very chaotic. Soldiers were yelling and screaming all over the place. Medics had already arrived before us, assisting to the wounded. I remember looking at one soldier, lying there, apparently dead. There were a lot of troops injured. Blood seemed everywhere. As I looked around, some of the soldiers in my platoon were just frozen at the sight of what they saw. Others rushed in to help where they could.

I immediately went to an injured soldier, who was leaning up against a tree and helped him the best I could. I had no medical training, except for a basic lifesaving class we had a few days earlier. I just tried to cover his wounds the best I could and keep him calm. His injuries didn't seem too bad. Emergency medical vehicles and choppers began to arrive and evacuate the wounded. Once the scene was stabilized, we were gathered back into formation, and we made the long journey back to our barracks. No one said a word. We were all in a daze.

Once back at the barracks, some soldiers in our platoon just broke down. A couple soldiers freaked out. The Platoon leader and Drill Sergeants quickly gathered up the soldiers that were having issues and took them away. We were told they would be sent to see counselors that would try and help them understand what had happened. Most of those soldiers I never saw again. We later heard that most were given immediate discharges. They could not handle it. We were close to completing our basic training, but that early in the military; I guess just some persons can't deal with traumatic events. It affected me as well. I still have nightmares about it, to this day.

Because of the accident, our basic training class was put on hold, to allow for an investigation, allow memorial services to be performed and such.

Once our training had resumed, everyone remained in a somber mood. Our Drill Instructors did everything they could to keep us focused, but it was difficult. While the cause of the investigation had not been officially released until much later, early on we heard it resulted from a Howitzer gun pointed incorrectly and was not properly checked before firing. And as a secondary cause, we were told that the powder charge in the weapon was too large for the round and target, which in turn caused the shot to travel at least 2KM further than it was intended to. I later learned that a similar accident had occurred at this range several months earlier.

Since this accident, I have learned that the particular artillery range where these rounds were fired from has been closed and relocated much, much further away, as to eliminate these type of tragedies from happening again. I would like to visit that location again someday, just to pay my respects for the fallen and injured.

As you can see from the two stories above, I have had some experiences in my life have had an affect me. I have found ways to deal with these experiences, and others I have endured throughout my life. Not all traumatic events must involve seeing someone getting wounded or killed. Battered spouses, rape victims, victims of child abuse, first responders, can have some form of PTSD. The typical stereotype out there is only combat soldiers can have or get PTSD, and that is simply not true. While I will never forget the things I have seen or experienced, I have found ways to deal with them so I can live my life in the most productive way I can.

The road to recovery and being able to live with PTSD starts with identifying what PTSD is, what the symptoms are, accepting that it is ok to have it, where you can get help, and then learning coping strategies for yourself and loved ones. You can live with PTSD. I know it may seem impossible, but you can do it.

Chapter 1: What is PTSD?

PTSD or Post-Traumatic Stress Disorder can be defined as a mental illness that is commonly set off by a shocking or frightening experience. A person may acquire post-traumatic stress disorder either by personally experiencing the trauma or simply being a witness. The usual symptoms of PTSD are constant nightmares, flashbacks of the terrifying experience, extreme anxiety and thoughts about the situation or episode which the patient cannot seem to control.

Many people who experience shocking or traumatic experiences may find it difficult to adjust and cope for a short time, the majority do not have PTSD. When these people are given enough time to recover and perform excellent self-care exercises, they can usually feel better after a short while. If the signs and symptoms become worse or continue for several months or even years and they start to get in the way of a person's normal day to day activities, then that person may be suffering from PTSD. If this is the case for you, you must be professionally diagnosed and treated for your symptoms by a certified physician. Once you begin treatment, you can lessen the signs and symptoms, and you can go back to a healthy lifestyle.

WHAT ARE THE SIGNS AND SYMPTOMS OF PTSD?

The signs and symptoms of PTSD usually begin within 3 months of the disturbing experience. Some people may not experience the symptoms until after several years later. The symptoms of PTSD can lead to considerable problems and issues not only in your work or social life but in your personal relationships. The signs and symptoms of PTSD can be classified into four categories: disturbing memories, evasion, transformations in your moods and thoughts and changes in your emotional responses.

DISTURBING MEMORIES

- Recurring and unwelcome memories of the shocking experience that distress you

- Flashbacks or the revival of the shocking experience as if it is occurring again

- Distressing dreams related to the traumatic experience

- Extreme emotional anguish or physical responses to things that remind you of the experience.

EVASION

- Attempting to evade recalling, talking about or even thinking about the traumatic experience

- Staying away from the people, activities and locations that remind you of the traumatic experience.

TRANSFORMATIONS IN YOUR MOODS

- Unconstructive or even harmful feelings about your own self or others

- Not feeling positive or optimistic emotions

- Losing interest and enjoyment in activities you previously took pleasure in.

- Feeling hopeless about the future

- Issues with memory that include inability to remember vital parts of the traumatic experience

- Having problems in sustaining intimate personal relationships

CHANGES IN YOUR EMOTIONAL RESPONSES

- Bad temper, anger flare-ups or even aggressive or violent behaviors

- Always being extra alert for any dangers

- Overpowering shame or guilt

- Behaviors that are self-destructive like excessive drinking or driving a car fast

- Problems with concentration

- Problems with sleeping

- Can be easily troubled, frightened, shocked or startled

- Intensity of Signs and Symptoms

The intensity of the signs and symptoms of post-traumatic stress disorder can fluctuate or change over time. The signs and symptoms may seem more apparent when experiencing stressful situations or when you come across things or people that remind you of your traumatic experience. For instance, when a person suffering from PTSD hears a vehicle backfire, he or she may remember his or her traumatic experiences during combat, or similar incident. When a rape victim is suffering from PTSD, he or she may feel overwhelming emotions upon seeing a news report about another victim of sexual assault. The other victim's experiences may make he or she remember his or her own painful memories.

WHEN SHOULD YOU CONSULT

YOUR DOCTOR?

Consider consulting a doctor when you experience troubling thoughts and emotions connected to your traumatic experience for more than one to two months. But if you sense that your signs and symptoms are becoming severe, and you are finding it difficult to be in control of your life again after the traumatic experience, you should not wait one month to consider seeing a mental health expert. Seeking early treatment and help can assist in preventing the signs and symptoms of your post-traumatic stress disorder from becoming worse.

SUICIDAL THOUGHTS

SUICIDAL THOUGHTS SHOULD NOT BE IGNORED OR DISREGARDED. IF YOU ARE HAVING THEM OR YOU KNOW SOMEONE WHO DOES, MAKE SURE THAT YOU SEEK HELP IMMEDIATELY THROUGH ANY OF THE FOLLOWING:

- Talk to your spouse, or a loved one or a close friend whom you trust.

- Call your spiritual leader or minister or anyone from your religious community.

- Call the hotline number (800-273-TALK or 800-273-8255) to talk to a trained counselor from the National Suicide Prevention Lifeline. These people are experts and are well-trained in dealing with these situations. You can also opt to contact the Veterans Crisis Line by dialing the same number and pressing 1.

- Set an appointment schedule with your family doctor or any mental health experts or any local health care professionals.

AGAIN, IF YOU BELIEVE THAT YOU HAVE STRONG DESIRES TO ATTEMPT COMMITTING SUICIDE OR IF YOU HAVE ALREADY HURT YOURSELF, IMMEDIATELY CONTACT 911 TO SEEK EMERGENCY HELP.

If you know someone with suicidal tendencies and have communicated his or her plan of carrying out suicide, you must ensure that he or she is always accompanied by another person and that he or she is never left all alone. Contact 911 right away or if it is possible to do so, bring the person to the emergency room of your local hospital.

Chapter 2: Common Causes of PTSD

You can acquire PTSD when you have experienced a situation that involves actual or even threatened death, severe injuries or violation of your sexuality. But there were also instances when a person acquires the disorder even when he or she merely observed or learned about these traumatic events. Medical experts do not have any conclusive causes for PTSD, yet some patients acquire the disorder for other reasons other than what is detailed above. Similar to the majority of other mental health disorders, PTSD most likely results from a complex mixture of these factors:

- Hereditary risks for mental illnesses like higher risks for depression and anxiety.

- Various life experiences and events such as the amount and gravity of traumatic experiences that the patient has gone through from the time when he or she is a small child.

- The person's temperament or the hereditary features of his or her personality.

- The brain's ability to regulate the hormones and chemicals that your body produces as a reaction to stress.

RISK FACTORS

Anyone, no matter what age, can acquire PTSD, however, certain risk factors can make some people more prone to acquire post-traumatic stress disorder after experiencing a traumatic situation than others. These risk factors include but are not limited to:

- Experiences of extreme or long-term trauma such as extended combat duty, working rotations in the emergency room, etc.

- Previous traumatic experiences that occurred while the person was still very young such as child abuse or abandonment.

- Being in a job that intensifies the person's risks of exposure to traumatic situations. First responders and military personnel who go out on combat missions have increased risks of post-traumatic stress disorder.

- The existence of other mental health issues such as depression and anxiety.

- Lack of a stable support system that involves loved ones and close friends.

- People with biological relatives who suffer from mental health issues also have higher risks of acquiring post-traumatic stress disorder.

TYPES OF TRAUMATIC EVENTS

Some of the most common traumatic events that frequently lead to the progression of PTSD include:

- Exposure to combat

- Neglect or abandonment during childhood

- Physical abuse during childhood

- Physical attacks

- Witnessing horrific events or death

- Sexual assault

- Being threatened by another person using a weapon

Aside from the traumatic events listed above, other situations or events can cause PTSD including natural disasters, fires, mugging, car accidents, robberies, torture, plane crash, kidnappings, terrorist attacks, receiving a medical diagnosis that is life-threatening and other intense or grave situations.

COMPLICATIONS OF PTSD

The signs and symptoms of PTSD often result in disruptions in the whole life of a person. It can affect his or her work, personal relationships, physical health, and enjoyment and satisfaction in the day to day activities. When you have PTSD, it can intensify your risks of acquiring other mental health disorders including anxiety, depression, eating problems, drug, alcohol and other substance abuse, and suicidal thoughts and behaviors.

Chapter 3: Seeking Help

If you think you have the signs and symptoms of PTSD, you should seek immediate help by consulting your family doctor or going directly to a mental health expert. Here is some information that can assist you in preparing for your doctor's appointment and what your expectations can be during the consultation.

Before you go to your doctor for the consultation, it would be ideal for you to write down these items, so you will not forget:

- The signs and symptoms you have observed in yourself and the length of time since you noticed them.

- Your personal details and information regarding any experiences or situations where you felt intense fears, horror, or feeling helpless. Include traumatic experiences even if they occurred a long time ago.

This information will be very helpful for your doctor in determining a potential root cause for what you are feeling.

It would be best if you can bring a loved one or a close friend with you when you consult your doctor. He or she will be very helpful in remembering all the information that your doctor will give you. Aside from your personal details and information, it is also ideal if you can write down the questions you want to raise during your consultation with the doctor. Here are some of the usual questions that PSTD patients should ask their doctors:

- What do you think are the causes of the signs and symptoms I am experiencing?

- Aside from PTSD, do you think there are other likely causes for my symptoms?

- What steps will you take to establish your diagnosis for my case?

- Do you think that my symptoms are only temporary or will they last for a longer period of time?

- What are the typical treatments you suggest for post-traumatic stress disorder?

- What can I do to handle the symptoms of my PTSD that will not affect my other existing health issues?

- When can I expect any improvements in my signs and symptoms?

- Do you think that I have increased risks for other mental health disorders because of my PTSD?

- Do you have any recommendations on what adjustments I must make both at home and at work to promote my faster recovery?

- Do you think it will be helpful for me to inform my colleagues at work about my condition?

- Will you be able to give me any reading materials on post-traumatic stress disorder? Which particular online sites do you suggest I visit?

You can add more questions to this list so you can clarify anything about PTSD you do not understand.

WHAT YOU CAN EXPECT DURING YOUR CONSULTATION WITH THE DOCTOR.

You can expect that your doctor will ask several questions to better understand your condition. For you to save time during the interview, it is ideal for you to prepare yourself for the possible questions that your doctor may ask. Some questions the doctor may ask:

- What signs and symptoms have you observed?

- Have your loved ones observed you exhibiting these signs and symptoms? If yes, when did they notice them?

- Have you witnessed or personally experienced a situation threatening to your own life or to someone else's?

- Have you ever been harmed emotionally, sexually or physically? This may be a difficult question for some. If you are with a loved one and feel reluctant to answer this in front of them. It is ok to ask them to leave the room for a few minutes so you can discuss with the doctor alone.

- Do you have any troubling memories, thoughts or nightmares of any traumatic experiences you have gone through?

- Have you felt like you were experiencing the traumatic experiences again and again through hallucinations or flashbacks?

- Do you stay away from specific places, people or situations that may cause you to remember the traumatic event?

- Do you feel like you have lost interest in activities and things you previously enjoyed?

- You do you feel like you have become emotionally numb?

- Do you feel on guard, jumpy or readily distressed?

- Do you frequently become irritated or angry?

- Do you have any sleeping troubles?

- Do you feel like there are existing events in your life that make you feel as if your life were in danger?

- Do you have any issues with your relationships both at home and at work?

- Do thoughts of bringing harm to yourself or to other people cross your mind?

- Do you take illicit substances or do you consume alcoholic beverages? If so, how frequently?

- Have you received any previous treatment for any symptoms of a psychiatric condition or have you been previously diagnosed with a mental disorder? If yes, which specific treatments do you think were most effective to you?

TESTING AND DIAGNOSIS

Your doctor will make his or her diagnosis based on the signs and symptoms you presented and through a comprehensive evaluation of your psychological condition. Aside from the interview questions, your doctor may request you to undergo a physical examination to see if you have other medical issues that may be causing your signs and symptoms.

Your doctor will only give a diagnosis of post-traumatic stress disorder if you met the criteria provided by the American Psychiatric Association in the Diagnostic and Statistical Manual of Mental Disorders or DSM-5. The DSM-5 is used by all mental health experts in the United States in diagnosing mental disorders and by insurance companies in reimbursing treatment costs. If you do not meet the standards for DSM-5, you may still be given a diagnosis and recommended treatments of other conditions such as depression or anxiety.

THE DSM-5 CRITERIA FOR POST-TRAUMATIC STRESS DISORDER

The DSM-5 criteria for the diagnosis of PTSD includes:

- You personally went through a traumatic experience.

- You were a personal witness of a traumatic experience.

- You found out that a person close to you went through or was endangered by a traumatic situation.

- You were exposed repetitively to vivid and realistic details of a traumatic event.

You also must have experienced one or more symptoms below after you have gone through the traumatic situation:

- You relive your traumatic experiences through disturbing visions and memories.

- You experience troubling dreams related to the traumatic situation.

- You encounter flashbacks as if you are going through the traumatic situation repeatedly.

- You go through continuing or severe emotional anguish or physical indications when you remember the traumatic situation.

You may also have experienced these symptoms for over a month after your traumatic experience:

- Trying to stay away from things, places or situations that prompt you to remember your traumatic experience.

- Not recalling vital aspects of the traumatic experience.

- Viewing yourself, other people or the entire world in a negative manner.

- Losing interest in things you previously enjoyed.

- Feeling detached from your loved ones and friends.

- Feeling emotionally numb.

- Increased irritability or angry outbursts.

- Engaging in activities or behaviors that are harmful to your own self or to other people.

- Sleeping or concentration problems.

- Becoming extra alert for indications of dangers.

- The signs and symptoms of the PTSD should be causing considerable anguish in your day to day living, and they hinder your capability to perform your regular activities.

Chapter 4: Common Treatment Methods

Getting treatment for your PTSD can aid you in regaining control of your own life. The initial treatment that your doctor may recommend is psychotherapy, but you may also be required to take certain medications. The combination of psychotherapy and medications can aid in improving the symptoms you experience, in teaching you certain skills that can help you manage your symptoms, and in helping you gain a better perspective of yourself. These two treatments can also assist in treating other health conditions that may have arisen from the traumatic event including anxiety, substance abuse and depression.

PSYCHOTHERAPY

Various types psychotherapy methods can be employed in treating PTSD in both kids and adults.

Cognitive therapy aims to help you identify your own thinking or cognitive patterns causing you to be trapped in your past experience. Cognitive therapy is typically employed combined with exposure therapy in treating PTSD.

Exposure therapy can aid you in safely facing the things you fear so you can learn how to deal with them positively and effectively. One technique of exposure therapy employs a "virtual reality" program that can let you go back to the traumatic situation.

Eye Movement Desensitization and Reprocessing, or EMDR, is a combination of exposure therapy and a sequence of guided eye movements which aims to assist you in processing your memories that are traumatic. The therapy can also help you alter your reactions to those traumatic recollections.

These techniques can assist you in gaining control of the fears left behind by your traumatic experience. You can work with your doctor to determine which particular approach will work for your specific needs. You can opt to undergo the therapies on your own, or you can join a group session, or you can have a combination of both.

MEDICATIONS

Usually, when diagnosed with PTSD, doctors will prescribe antidepressants to treat anxiety and depression. You may be asked to take them if you experience concentration or sleeping problems. The FDA has approved the prescription of Zoloft (sertraline) and Paxil (paroxetine) which are both SSRIs, or selective serotonin reuptake inhibitors to treat PTSD. Let your doctor know of any health issues or medications not previously disclosed before taking antidepressants.

You may also be asked to take anti-anxiety drugs which can aid in temporarily improving your stress and anxieties. You will only be asked to take these medicines for a short period of time because they are conducive to abuse with long-term use.

If you experience insomnia or recurring nightmares, your doctor may prescribe Minipress (prazosin) to help you sleep better.

Similar to psychotherapy, you also must closely work with your doctor in determining which particular medication will work best for your situation. You can expect improvements in your overall mood after a couple of weeks of medication intake. If you experience any side effects, make sure that you immediately inform your doctor, so he or she adjust your prescription or prescribe an alternative.

No matter what, take no medication not prescribed to you and always follow the prescription to the letter. Never consume alcohol while taking the medications, as it will have an adverse effect.

Chapter 5: Coping Techniques

These techniques may be useful in helping you cope with the symptoms of PTSD while you are undergoing psychotherapy and other treatments.

Strictly adhere to the treatment plan prescribed to you by your doctor. You must realize that your PTSD symptoms will not disappear overnight. You may need to wait for a couple of weeks after the start of your treatments before you can see any noticeable improvements. Do not feel impatient and always remind yourself to strictly adhere to your prescribed treatment plan.

Learn more about post-traumatic stress disorder. When you better understand what you are going through, you can create your own coping techniques that will help you to deal with your symptoms. Involve your family members in the learning process. The more people around you that understand PTSD, the more success they will have in helping you cope.

Make sure that you are taking good care of yourself. Eat a healthy diet and exercise regularly. Give yourself enough time to sleep at night and sufficient time to relax. Stay away from addictive behaviors such as smoking and drinking alcohol because they can worsen your PTSD symptoms, and have an adverse effect on your mood and health.

When feeling angry, afraid or anxious, ask yourself to take a break and go for a quick walk until you can re-focus your attention.

Sustain your personal relationships. Make sure that you can regularly talk with your family and friends about what you are feeling. You need not go into the details, just an overview is typically enough for them to understand. Just being with people who care about you and who support you can greatly help in your healing and recovery.

WHEN A LOVED ONE HAS PTSD

This section is for the caregivers. It will provide you with some guidance in helping the one you care about deal with PTSD.

You may notice that your loved one, a spouse or a family member, has become different after experiencing a traumatic event. This is most commonly seen after a person serving in the military returns from a deployment. You may notice he or she has become more irritable, angry, depressed or withdrawn. You must realize that PTSD is not their fault. PTSD can cause considerable damage personal relationships, mainly due to the lack of understanding by those not suffering from it. You may notice that your loved one wants to talk about the experience, yet it's hard for them to explain the details, so they may begin to talk and then suddenly stop and close everything off again. You may feel hopeless that the person you love can get help. You may feel guilt and helplessness for not being able to make things right for your loved one, or you cannot speed up his or her healing process. Always remind yourself there are things you can do to help.

First, try to learn more about PTSD so you can better understand what your spouse or family member is experiencing.

Realize that withdrawal is a symptom of PTSD. If your loved one refuses the support you give, give him enough space while letting them know that you will always be there for them when he or she is prepared to receive your support.

Offer to come with them when going to the doctor office. Going with your loved one to the physician will enable you to better understand his or her condition and how you can help in the healing process.

Have the willingness to listen. Make sure that your loved one knows that you will always be there to listen and that you understand if he or she doesn't wish to talk sometimes, it's ok.

Involve your loved ones in activities which will enable him or her to reconnect with other people.

CAN PTSD BE PREVENTED?

It is normal for people to experience symptoms that are similar to PTSD after enduring a traumatic experience. If you have just suffered a serious car accident, for example, it is normal for you to not to be able to stop your thoughts about the crash.

Anxieties, guilt, fears, depression and even anger are all natural responses to a traumatic event. Most people who experience a traumatic event do not acquire lasting PTSD symptoms.

Seeking immediate help and support are critical to helping prevent long-lasting effects of a traumatic event. You must find the courage to look for the help and support of your loved ones and family.

You may even consider consulting a mental health expert to see if there is a brief therapy you can take to help you cope. Other people find it very helpful when they seek support from their religious community. Always remember that it is possible to control the problem before it becomes worse and develops into a full-blown post-traumatic stress disorder. If you feel you have PTSD, don't let the stigma get in your way. There is always help to those who seek it.

Chapter 6: Living with PTSD

Living with PTSD can be a daily struggle. The smallest things can set off the symptoms. Fireworks, rush hour, packed shopping malls, even little things like a telemarketing call can set them off. Another challenge in living with PTSD is most people that have never experienced it, or even heard of it, have a hard time understanding or believing in the condition. Sometimes this can even can exacerbate the stress and create additional anxiety with those who are affected as they feel they constantly must quantify their feelings and emotions.

Due to the recent sacrifices of the US military and spouses, resulting from extended deployments and combat actions around the globe, PTSD is becoming more accepted as a valid condition. The truth is, PTSD as a condition has been around for decades. During the WW II, it was called shell shock. During the Vietnam War, it was known as Combat Stress. The next level of education for the public is to show that PTSD can occur in many other places other than the military.

We all can help those affected by PTSD. However, any successful treatment begins at home. We spend most of our time in our homes and around loved ones, so it is reasonable to ascertain that creating a warming, stable and stress-free home life helps PTSD sufferers cope and live happy and productive lives.

Earlier in this book, strictly adhere to the treatment plan prescribed to you. Keeping your focus can be difficult. Lean on family members for support and help keep you on track.

Remove any triggers from within your home. Such things as bright colors, colored lights, unnecessary items in rooms such as too much furniture, all can be triggers. Certain colors such as red can cause aggressive behaviors and/or tendencies. Try changing colors to neutral or blue colors for a more calming effect. Having too many items in a room can make you feel crowded and restricted.

Try to avoid high-stress situations such as traffic jams. We have all sat in bumper to bumper traffic and have experienced those inconsiderate drivers that feel they own the road. This can cause anger emotions and aggressive tendencies. Work with your employer and see if you can change your hours to help avoid the busy traffic times or see if a position change would allow you to telecommute. Don't be ashamed in involving your employer as part of your support system.

We spend at least half of our week at our job. The employer should be a part of the solution, not part the problem. If the employer doesn't help, then it may be time to consider looking for employment elsewhere.

If your PTSD has progressed to where your personal life is experiencing challenges such as abuse, divorce, or child custody issues, make sure you take some time for yourself. Treat yourself to a massage, or a haircut. Get away from the situation when you feel overwhelmed. With divorce and other issues, just remember, it may be tough, but it will get better. Above all, remember, while you are the one suffering from PTSD, your loved ones can be affected by your actions.

Be respectful and appreciative of them. They are there to help.

Get plenty of exercise. Even if your PTSD resulted from combat, and you may even have substantial physical wounds resulting from your duty, still try and exercise and rehab yourself. Exercise lowers blood pressure and reduces stress dramatically.

Sleep, sleep, sleep. Getting rest may seem like a simple thing, but sufferers of PTSD normally have a hard time getting to sleep and or staying asleep. Every effort should be made to give yourself an inviting and stress-free place to rest. Televisions should be removed from bedrooms, put in blackout curtains, try a sound machine that can provide soothing sounds such as the ocean, can all provide an inviting place to rest and sleep. If you have a hard time staying asleep, and you find the ocean sounds help you get to sleep, consider having the sound machine run all night. Get as much rest as you can. There should not be any set number of hours required. Your body and mind will tell you when it is rested. You should not, however, rely on medications to put you to sleep. These drugs, while they help in getting to sleep, they will not provide your body the required sound rest you need. Give yourself a before bed ritual such as a nice soak in the tub, or a massaging shower. I will venture to say, sleep is one most important aspect of any PTSD treatment. There is way too much technology these days. We all must disconnect from our phone and tablets and give ourselves rest.

Finally, if you snore heavily, a CPAP machine may be the answer. Consult with your doctor about treatment options for snoring. Many people have had great success with CPAP machines to relieve their snoring, hence giving them a more restful sleep.

Stay away from drugs and alcohol. If you are on prescribed medications, please adhere to your prescribed doses. Consult with your doctor if the medications are affecting your sleep or making you feel aggressive. Also, consult with them on the plan to wean you off of the medications when your treatment is complete. Ask your doctor about what are the milestones that need to be met that begin a phased reduction and elimination of your medications.

No medications are ever designed to be long term or permanent solutions except a few such as insulin or some thyroid medications. No matter what the situation, alcohol should never be part of your treatment plan and recovery. If you an alcoholic, there is help out there to assist you in eliminating your desire for it. Alcohol is one of the biggest trigger enhancers for PTSD. It causes us to be more aggressive, more emotional, and to feel more invincible. Remove all sources of alcohol in your home, to include anything that advertises it. Have a garage sale. If garage sales are too stressful, then give it to a friend or relative to sell at theirs.

Provide help and support to other local PTSD organizations in your area. There are support organizations in virtually every city and town. Providing help and support to others who can relate to you can assist you in ways you cannot imagine. You will be around people who can relate to your condition, connect with your experiences, and feel comfortable in talking with you. Maybe something you have learned to help you deal with your situation can help someone else out there who is struggling.

Look into getting a service dog. Even of the dog is not professionally trained as a service dog, many breeds of dog out there have a calm demeanor. Dogs are very loyal companions and have abilities to sense when we are having emotional issues and even some medical issues. My dog, a boxer, never trained, always seems to know when I am stressed or upset, and just comes over and places his head in my lap, as to tell me it's ok and he is there for me.

Similar to canine help, equine therapy has also been shown to dramatically reduce stress and anxiety. More facilities are opening up that specialize in equine therapy. Look into it.

Just remember, staying away from stressful situations, making a comfortable home environment and surrounding yourself with people who care about you will go a long way in helping you cope. You will never forget the experiences you endured or the tragedies you encountered. They will always be a part of you and your memories. Together, we can learn how we can control them, and not let them control us.

Conclusion

I hope that this book provided you with some direction in determining if you or someone you care for, possibly has PTSD, and some of the treatment and coping methods involved in helping them. Numerous studies are being conducted both in the military medical community and the civilian community on better testing, diagnosis, and treatments for all forms of PTSD. I encourage all sufferers of PTSD to participate in these studies so doctors can better understand how to treat it.

REMEMBER, YOU ARE NOT ALONE!

If you are reading this book and feel as though you are in a similar situation, the end of your rope, please look for help.

In the last 30 years, a lot has changed regarding technology and resources. There are people and organizations out there that can and will help you. All it takes is the courage to get away from dangerous situations and call for help. Here are a few resources you can call right now. Don't wait until it is too late.

If you feel you are in a dire situation, please dial 911 NOW! They will dispatch the police or ambulance right away.

National Suicide Hotline U.S.- 1 (800) 273-8255 – If you feel like you have nowhere to turn and even have remote thoughts of ending your life, please call this number. Just remember, there are people out there that care for you and would not want to see you hurt or worse. Think about the impact to them if something happens to you.

Veteran Crisis Hotline 1.800.273.TALK (8255) If you are an active service member or veteran, call the PTSD Foundation of America. They can help with any issues you may be facing, whether it is related to PTSD or not.

National Sexual Assault Hotline - 1.800.656.HOPE (4673) – As a part of the RAINN network, (RAPE, ABUSE, and Incest National Network), you can call this number and get help. Over 1000 volunteers are on call at any given time.

National Runaway Safe Line – **1.800.786.2929** – If you are a runaway, or you know someone who is, please call. They will help you in keeping safe and get you off the streets. Parents and adults, you can call to get more information and to report a runaway.

Your Mother, Father, Brother, Sister, Aunt, Uncle or Best Friend. Call someone. If you don't make the call, no one can help.

DID YOU ENJOY THIS BOOK?

Thank you for purchasing and reading this book. I hope it helped you understand what PTSD is all about, how to identify it, and how to cope and live a happier life with it. I know it is not a long book. It was not intended to be. I didn't want to fill it with excess information to overwhelm you. If you are looking for a more comprehensive guide on PTSD, look at the titles above and or below this one in Amazon. I am sure there is one there for you.

Just remember, you are not alone. There are resources out there to help you. I know it may be difficult to ask for help, but it is out there.

Can I ask a quick favor?

If you enjoyed this book, I would appreciate it if you could leave me a positive review on Amazon.

I love getting feedback from my readers, and reviews on Amazon do make a difference. I read all my reviews and would appreciate your thoughts.

Thanks so much.

John Mackey

Author

U.S. Army, Desert Storm Veteran

PTSD sufferer

About the Author

John Mackey is a decorated U.S. Army, Desert Storm veteran. John served for 8 years within the continental U.S. and overseas. John's hobbies comprise astrophotography and being an author. John is also a successful business owner in the Information Technology field. He takes great pride in helping his customers operate their businesses.

As an author, John enjoys writing about modern and current events that can affect everyday lives. John is always researching topics for new books and continually edits his existing books to ensure the content is up to date and accurate.

Manufactured by Amazon.ca
Bolton, ON